FOURTH FLOOR FLAT

# FOURTH FLOOR FLAT
*44 Cantos*

Terry McDonagh

ARLEN
HOUSE

*Fourth Floor Flat*

is published in 2018 by
ARLEN HOUSE
42 Grange Abbey Road
Baldoyle
Dublin 13
Ireland
Phone: 353 86 8360236
Email: arlenhouse@gmail.com
arlenhouse.blogspot.com


Distributed internationally by
SYRACUSE UNIVERSITY PRESS
621 Skytop Road, Suite 110
Syracuse, NY 13244–5290
Phone: 315–443–5534/Fax: 315–443–5545
Email: supress@syr.edu


978–1–85132–170–4, paperback

Typesetting by Arlen House

Cover image by Sally McKenna
and Studio Macha

Printed and bound in the UK by
ImprintDigital.com

# CONTENTS

*In memory of Philip Casey*
*friend, poet and novelist*

# FOURTH FLOOR FLAT

Thinking: *the talking of the soul with itself*
　　　　　　　　　　　　　　　　　　　– Plato

The mind is bigger than the space we inhabit. The protagonist in this collection is the *Everyman* in us who leaves *the yowl and yelp of his home crowd* to shape a future – to distance himself from the familiar, so-called tried and tested. He finds his place, space and voice in a fourth floor flat from where, in 44 cantos, he grants us access to his hopes, dreams, expectations and thought patterns.

As we progress through the collection, we begin to realize that the human being cannot avoid thinking unusual, strange, confused, happy, absurd and ridiculous thoughts – and these thoughts or images present themselves consciously and unconsciously in orderly, chaotic, mumbo-jumbo chunks from birth to death.

How many images can the observer observe and process in an instant, an hour, a day? Almost impossible to answer, although some have tried with limited success. Of greater significance is the fact that this character opens up a window to the remarkable/unremarkable existence of one person – perhaps allowing us insight into our own incomplete, time-strapped world of work-in-progress.

Think we do, and think we must – to deny, avoid or ignore thinking is not an option.

　　　*Summer! it is summer*
　　　*– and still the roar in his mind is*
　　　*unabated*
　　　　　　　– William Carlos Williams

## SETTING OUT

Before broadband here, there
and everywhere,
a long-haired youth
slunk so far into foothills
that he lost sight of home
and home lost sight of him.

A glutton for pilgrim habits,
he traipsed and tracked
from land to land,
village, seashore and city
chasing star after elusive star
dreaming from inside out
considering a bond with
the devil and alien recipes
when he chanced upon a room
just a stone's throw
from a voice in first person
yet far enough from the yowl
and yelp of his home crowd.

At first he turned to his nag
wondering if it was best
not to have a *now* at all
but looking up at cloud pockets,
sunsets, life and half-life,
he knew he'd have to comment
on the underbelly of fortune
if only to blame – when suddenly
out of the blue like
a whole shebang of
hammer and tongs
in a gutful of pig iron,
he blurted out
from his high horse:

*I will.*
*Words are mine.*
*Mine to speak.*

I'M HERE NOW

That past of mine was quirked,
discordant, full of black wind
but it is history, impetuosity
and so last year. I could shout
*come back youth*
but that's as futile as near kisses
and whinging – the heart asks joy.

I'm content on the fourth floor
but think I could be happy
in a wilderness of rock pool,
gorse, hawthorn and hazel,
a place where plant touches plant,
songbirds focus the sun – where
I'd be free to go round in circles.

Up here I flick through day and dark
in the wriggling world of witchcraft,
homespun yoga and hymns of
jerky homage to a lost youth.

Night has lodged in my bloodstream
and road is spinning and shedding
all around me – I crave calm – silence.

In the mood for a snack, that's me
but I'm clean out – my last biscuit
a silhouette – my cupboard quiet
and mocking: *diet, diet*
*it's your call*
*who's the skinniest of them all?*

What's natural isn't wonderful
isn't much of an answer

but tell me
where is the magic pool
or dancer on sparkling donkey back
that points to where thinking is located?

God doesn't reply, so maybe
when sloes are ripening and
bees are out in summer finery
I'll get in touch with imps and elves
to learn more about brazen winds
that have so much say
in songs we sing or screams we scream
as lights crash into each other after dark.

## ON A ROLL

Because I know it's there
I stroke my balding patch
as my friend, Mouse,
nibbles away in the corner
in ways known to mice.

I'm on a roll. Radio and me
going full blast with versions
of *I Can't Get No Satisfaction.*
Then without change of pace
I snap my eyes shut, jump
into a jig with a gaggle of geese
and an academy of high-stepping
hilltop antelopes – me twisting,
jiving like a coy thing in my
own space. *Stop staring Mouse.*
*Come to my grove if you've got*
*jingle-jangle feet to jig on.*

I clap myself on the back, rile
and yell a few times. Mouse
has done with crumbs and left.
I turn to my feet for guidance.
They look up and I look down.
We try an awkward Ali shuffle
routine sort of thing before
diving into weed and fantasy.

The starting gun won't give up.
Tired as an old fish fighting tides
I plonk into a chair,
place my flat hand on my jaw
and pose, yearning to inhabit
a houseful of thoughts – formulae
for an opus – knowing

I'm no longer the youth
I left wounded and short of guts
in a field of fresh spuds.
The flat of my hand still rests on my jaw.

I prowl, open the kitchen window
to the disgruntle of a jackhammer
while down at the next corner
a deaf, near-sighted violinist
with eyes for heroes only
scrapes a requiem to lost legions
in rough wind. There must
have been a hint of hope for him
before battle and grimy time
swallowed up his idols but
he will play till his terror fades
into his playing. I pick up on
his howl and shut the window.

## HOLY JESTING

In spite of the grace of god, imams
and prelates, I'm still only a tenant
aching to be a charmer and
fearless minder of word – might
even be a legate on a pedestal
with armfuls of incantations
exhorting eruptions to sprinkle
purple dust and folk karma
on the greedy. Let's hymn together.
Amen.
If sheep and lambs followed me
I'd have a flock to turn to.
I'm told I'm a ringer for a singer
strident among briars and berries
but I'm not just a singer – I'm a
scribbler under house arrest
in a sanctuary of hard limestone
and soundbites without a whisker
of a vesper to my name. There are
rough drafts at large as we speak
and, if needs be, I'll roam with gypsy
and blackbird to snatch pure chant
off the horizon. *Hang on, Mouse,*
*there's more to come:* bishop, imam
high up and tall, who's the sexiest of
them all? *I am* whispered the woman
on high and all in *his* head. Oh, Oh!

Holy Joes in costume are a howl.
No blood left, hallow as bamboo
and just look at the getup of them
in daylight – bag ladies with no bags.
Some write psalms in secret and
hide sisters in grim grey to black
to knee and full length, who grin,

bear, manage the club, buy buns
for paradise parties or the four-poster.
*Give you a kick in the privates,*
*ye auld codger,* said she after prayer
and fasting. Don't know how he
responded but I'd have outed, *oops*
or *careful lady.*

I'm at home in a foreign place
without parrot or prayer
to remind me of far-off fantasies.
I inhabit these seasoned streets
like a swallow that comes and goes.

*Evening sir, could I interest you*
*in a tasty bird?* What if a sprig
of homeland spirits were to tune in?
Ah, I'm giving myself the creeps.
I'm here and know so little. Perhaps
it's time to take a blind leap of faith
into the corner of the next giggly breeze.

## SHENANIGANS

Thoughts can be disturbing,
flimsy, tatty – as disjointed
as wrack and ruin. You've
got them lined up, pensive
when out of the blue, words
like financial haircut, crash
or a few rounds of wallops
and dancing to corporate tunes
interrupt the stillness of silence.

From time to time, as foil against
the weary weight of gloom,
I'd take part in pub shenanigans
with youngish dreamers.
Some, innocent as oysters,
sparkled – others lamenting,
swore minor poets were lesser,
postmodern was passé
and Paddy loved pints. We'd
get ruddy, cheery and beveraged.

On one occasion a pale male,
having taken time to ponder
on a considered position
adopted by a young woman
in pink stilettos, plagiarized:
*unthrifty loveliness, why dost thou spend*
*upon thyself thy beauty's legacy?*
... Shakespeare Sonnet 4.

Motto: don't look back – ever!
Guinness, Guinness it's your call,
who's the latest to cringe by the wall.

Needless to say
we went our poetic ways.

## BUZZ AND BRAND

I'm afraid I don't have a buzz word,
Mr Commerce, but sun, moon and
rain don't either. If only you could
see me up here, you'd say, ah ha,
hold it right there – you'll need a
decent set of golf clubs and an
up to date six-pack to set you right.
You're a looney, a basket case,
a header in a tower without any
notion of noise. So let's dally in
the real world of brand and label,
even jazz up the Mother of God
if needs be – give her top ratings.
She'd not come cheap with her
in-house contacts, but let's face it,
it's all about fat loss, wink and
tongue muscle training, isn't it?

Mr Commerce, if you could
see my corpulent neighbour
scuttling the street below
I'd imagine you labelling
these unique features as
reincarnated throwbacks to
a previous life badly led
without image or add – could
even be extinct cherub or
dodo parts – alien bits on a lost ledge.

It's true, my neighbour won't model.
Could be a blow-in on a nightmare,
a manipulated food outlet, a daydreamer
trapped in caged, corporate air – but

you don't own up to nightmares, Mr C.
You trumpet, foghorn and flush
to still the mocking jigsaw under grass.

If I were asked for a buzz word
in noisy gym, rip and muscle time,
I'd be inclined to lean towards silence:
side-of-hill silence
deep valley silence
prayer-at-grave silence.

Saint Mary Magdalene
you know
I've always wanted to
be nothing other than
a high-flying singer
in a gush of notes
by a humming river bank.

## SOUR GRAPES

My time on planet earth
has been shaped by zig zag,
wild oats and sour grapes.

I'm in a fourth floor flat,
certain I'm being spied upon
by bishops with binoculars
on church steeples and
pigeons on rooftops when
I've only got my mortarboard,
the plotting moon, darkness,
daydream and my black hoodie
to protect me, so let's share
a few thoughts before the sun
gets up:
can I know if one wayward heartthrob
beats faster than another
next to a gorgeous glass of Merlot
or
can I convey my garbled version
of a nightmare flitting down
a holy mountain on horseback at sunrise
when all I do is turn to myself for solace?

Can't even connive with you
these days, a lover might say.
In such moments, turning to
an insurance broker for therapy
is pointless. I quiz myself,
have notions of doing romance
and giving myself forty lashes
until I consider the consequences.

The youth in me is getting stale.
If questioned by Revenue

I'd own up to being a minstrel
among cloud nine foothills
with experience of struggle
in human scrambling – using
only hands and feet – and I'd
insist I only wanted to channel
a few words into an opening line.
A scrapbook would be a start.
Well, that's what I say to myself.
To a uniform I might say, grand day.
I have glimpses of a first line.
Then none. Nothing. Zilch.

I try to envisage an assortment
of psychic threads – links to
vegan song lines, prisons, Rome,
Hindus, Buddhists, refugees or
children swinging on golden gates
and then my urge for sour grapes returns.

WISDOM

I sometimes wonder if
I followed the teachings
of the Vatican or the *Koran*
would I become wise
like a child is wise
like our dog is wise
like Socrates was wise?
When I offered my seat
to a blind man, he seemed
to look me through before
asking *what's the matter*
reminding me of a kind man
telling tales of a blind poet
on a hilltop before
*The Daily Mail* lined us up
like sitting ducks at a Christmas dinner.

A top story must include:
he's got twenty-four kids
doesn't know what he wants
might have the hots
for a best mate and one eye
on a spicy road leading
all the way to an altar of incense.

Can language sink so deep in trash
that we no longer hear the murmur
of a bee or the voice or a child
telling a teacher they understand
to keep education at arm's length?

As a boy dreamer, I'd imagine myself
a bleeding finger under a cold tap.
Flow-away-flow and me in the company
of Dracula in Transylvania.

At this moment I'd like to be alone
with Mouse on a hilltop of fairy lights
but I don't think I'll ever see that magical land
unveiling its wisdom in song and drum.

## ARMCHAIR

I've got this mighty armchair and
a bunch of greenery – planty things
on the low table in front of Buddha.
I'm fine – not a Buddhist
but I have read enough
and done tail flips with a Golden Fish.

If I hid and scavengers didn't hover
I might never be discovered but
I have my place to keep me in place.
My friend, Mouse, tidies up crumbs
and I sleep in the smaller room.
Twitches and commedia are confined
to this room or to the kitchen. It is said

Shakespeare's plays are dramatic
because most of the action
takes place elsewhere – almost
everywhere except on stage.
I've written a few books but
the Shakespearian breakthrough
has been avoiding me. I want to write,
I say. I say it again: *I'd love
to write a mighty novel.*
All if, but and hallucination.

This morning on the phone
about a reading tour, I said
I wouldn't budge without cash.
Lemming panic. Foamy noise
battering at rocky bits. I swore
my works were eager and edgy,
then blurted out: Marx says
all history is economic with
no guarantee of a kingdom come.

It was all over in a click.
Hosanna to blushing and hang ups.

Being quiet is fine, isn't it? Leaves
turn green in absolute silence.
The child of truth is always premature,
I concluded, with my head spinning
like a prima ballerina on something.

Oh yes, I do have ideas. I look down
into the street or across at a figure
that doesn't fret about curtains
and there you have a page or two.
I trundle down to the coffee shop
swaying to the rhythm of bird life,
feeling very much the artist
thinking about dropping a line to god.

I return to lie on my bed, get up,
gander, sit into my big flowery chair,
switch on the telly but that's about it.
What about the manuscript, you might ask.
I'm too wordy for theatre I'm told and
haven't got staying power for a novel.

I'm meeting a friend later to lean on a cliff barrier,
to chat about wellbeing, stray love and the like.
I've promised an epic. Heroic. Won't happen.
Too big. I think I won't be going anywhere
in a hurry, but you'd never know – my brain
is still loose enough to absorb outlandish noises.

THERAPY

I did therapy once, thinking
it might get me started – at what
I don't know – the valley
doesn't know what lies beyond.

I did therapy
to get my hands clapping
I did therapy.

The state tempted with sessions
to get me talking about myself
turning over old stones of disgrace.
I'd ring the front door bell, obey
the buzzer and waddle through to
a waiting room. The person, client
before me would exit elsewhere.
Doors to this and that – revolving
doors to other worlds. Alice!
If you walk through that dark door
you'll never arrive or return
in your tippy-toe-squeaky slip-ons.
Trapdoors. Low-life-hoodwinking.
Hush-hush-stuff.
I didn't let my therapist anywhere
near thorny tissues. No hammering
neat little love numbers on tables.
However, I did shriek a lot to cover up.

Just imagine the wealth of ideas
available to the novice novelist
if client notes could be plagarized.

Divide and conquer. Single rows
and we don't even touch, loping in
one door and revolving out another.

A question like: what tablet or
position on the scale of madness
are you on, would be an opener
or let's take our tales to a café,
discuss mother, lay libido bare and
bingo … a therapist is out of work
say I all smug. Forgive me, Mr Freud.
By the way, my friend is a therapist.
I love a laugh with fellow maniacs.

Back to the story: the door
to the inner chamber would
open mysteriously – a path
to a god and signal to step
forward into the chat cage.
*I'm all right Jack.* It was
one of those fantasy rooms
with thick walls. Not only
was there one door between
rooms – there were two with
breathing space in between.
When I suggested this gap
might be a hidey hole for
an escaping spirit, there was
an intake of breath. A silence.
I put on my shrine face.
In measured tones, I was asked
to take a seat in a ladylike
parlour armchair with wings.
Grand.
The therapist appraised, weighed,
suggested death played a role in
my troubled routine. I foiled, fended,
clung fists into the armrests hinting
I'd dabbled in Heidegger.

When I say dabbled, I mean dabbled.
I was quick to add that was the extent
of my knowledge but it didn't
affect me on a day-to-day basis
and I was a reasonable squash player.

We lost each other in a maze of
birdsong language and grave digging.
*Alas poor Yorick, I knew him well*
was my parting scream.
Yah, if only I'd met other clients,
I might be out of my deep dark place
and halfway through my *magnum opus*.

Aside: I wonder why we are clients,
cases and patients.
I feel white smoke coming on – is it
time to put my name on the waiting list
for an odyssey?

Therapy is a needle in a haystack
over drinks in establishments
when cultivating the hiding hands
of a special person. Are my fingers
younger than the rest of me? Oh oh!

I could have done dirges for Dorothy
I could have done laments for Lucy
I could have done chants for Chantelle.
I could have ... could have ... could have ... could ...

DISQUIET

Success is relative.
My room is cosy.
I'm on the top floor.
No one above me.
Any overhead noises
apart from jackdaws
scrapping over worms
would be of concern –
disquiet is the word
I'm searching for.
As the city darkens
I hear thunder and see
black cats staring as if
I was a turtle on the run
from raindrops.

Cats and turtles don't pay rent
and a residence far out at sea
is no solution either. Agents
will never turn their backs on
fat dinners by lapping shores,
or look twice at writers
wringing their hands – nor
can I imagine one of them
in a coracle at first light
armed with a lucrative contract
to be signed by the Messi of poetry
in exchange for a stash of cash and
a haven beyond the reach
of cranky critics. My heart
changes pace when I think
of reward. I did a sort of
empty-room-echo reading
in an art gallery for no money
and felt a spooky *déjá vu* when

the woman promised a crowd.
She had a mailing list and I
could sell books. Five showed up.
I was the guilty horse in harness
that couldn't pull a crowd. I sold
a book and downed the profits in a gulp.

Some milestones stand out
like green wind in a boggy field:
*would you like to read*
*along the Baltic coast?*
*Aye*, said I. The first, a pub
run by a poet-loving person,
came to nothing – no way
back – life must go on and
it did to an abandoned barge
at midnight with blazing lights
glaring me in the face and
a sparse gathering eyeballing
in spaced-out heavy-metal raptures.
My fee would be coming. It didn't.

## ICE CREAM

A far-fetched aside:
from inside this window,
I'm looking down
on a big tree
that reminds me
of a maverick ice cream cone
with branches reaching out
like singing firewood
like scallywagging arms.
Aside end.

## The Pub

You get more than your fill in pubs.
Some years ago
I was slurping away at a beer
when an acquaintance
windfell on to the high stool
next to me.
*How do you see yourself?*
says he.
Before I've time to answer
he suggests I no longer
see myself as a poet with a job.
Silence. It stung.
One leg over the other. More silence.

A song to silence.
A wounded west wind.
A song to silence.

His dad had something on the liver
while romance and the like
had scattered his family
round the globe – one out foreign,
another somewhere
and a divorcee at a distance.
He didn't volunteer details
on his father's lesion. The night
progressed – me toe-twitching,
my mind swaying, wondering
if beer could be an obstacle to love.
I got home late to the music
of black dogs
watching both ways for traffic.

Every situation has tipping points.
I sit them out and look to my hands:

not the hands of a bricklayer or
salt miner. They look soft – almost
infallible, fly-trapping gadgets.
I'm a bit hard on myself, I think, but
I am ignorant of palms and tea leaves.

I might sound like a man trying
to dabble in the dark arts
but no, I'm mainstream, nervy,
a carbon copy of the man
who never travelled without his
five-gallon drum in case
he ran dry a few kilometres out of town.

## ALL IN MY HEAD

There's a fellow down in the street
with a briefcase fastened to his bike
and he going hammer and tongs.
I wonder if he's an operator,
a peddler on a pair of wheels,
a Faustian slave – a hot-footer
leaving prison behind for the time being.

I'm at the window
as day makes way for evening.
Go to sleep, child in me.
Go far away
to places you have never been,
wrap yourself in trusted tales
and warm stories of childhood.

I loved *Swiss Family Robinson* and
*Robinson Crusoe* with his Man Friday.
I heard hoofbeats in cowboy comics.
There were mean men riding low,
guns blazing and

                              baddies

                  dropping

            like
flies.

A sheriff job would have been perfect
for me. I had a stray ass for a nag,
a homemade saddle of canvas
and fantasies in a marshy field.
This was no platform for hobos.
The saloon in the corner
under arching blackthorn was
brim full of gunslinging gals,
cowpokes and fearless men that

never turned a back on rustlers
or lost eye contact with batwing doors.

My steed had a mind of its own.
We covered miles of prairie,
always alert, doing good,
never more than half asleep
even when flat out under stars.
*Go for your guns. Lowdown critter.*
The bad stayed bad, got shot
or locked up thanks to me.
The good got wounded,
were rescued and tended to
by seasoned daughters who didn't cry.

I'd get dirty looks in the silent library.
The librarian was stern with a scary look
that made me blush, even when
I wasn't the one rattling her cage.

I'd gather feathers and arrows
for times when I was Chief
and feeling the need
to support my underlings.

Here I am wondering how
to get started
as evening creeps up
like a trapped frown.
I see a reflection of
the child in me out of
the corner of my eye
in the window pane
knowing that a toddler
doesn't give a hoot about books.

I have only one heart to care for
absorbed as I am in sounds of
absent-minded ghosts and people passing.

## AVOIDING TABLETS

Funny, we can't remember babyhood.
All that pre and toothless stuff and
not a trace left – *ah, for pity's sake!*

When a teenager went to the city
with his mother, she let go – had to,
with him shouting *it's not fair* – she
dodging the rain and they spinning.

Come to think of it, I didn't allow
my therapist this insight but I did
shout *freedom* and sing to myself
out of the twinkle of an eye.
Later, to avoid tablets I signed up
to a group session going round
in circles on heartstring songs,
shilly-shallies and herbal juices.

Loss of partner.
Gain of partner.
Looking at the moon.
Rounds of coquetry.

I was the hare on the back foot
itching in the wind
when
a pair of devastating eyes
expressed interest in a flirt.
Her partner had burst out
to go to the dogs – gone pious
and I had come from a circus.
*I have,* said I – sauntering.
In general, I'd have nothing
against sharing ding-a-ling
but breeze is breeze, wind

is wind and storm is exciting.
I prefer my own scars. I imagine
I must have feared erotic songs,
not that I begrudge erotisticians
their magical embrace – but I'd
never be able to add fresh flesh
to laundries on the subject. I do
like an occasional dream – coupling
life with forbidden – it's harder to
match up the living with the dead.

I'd often get well canned
till street lights took me
to glittered-up places. Bitter
sunrises – *feckin deadly*.

A day in the life of a person
freed-up from restraints and tablets
would be a great read – imagine
yourself hiding behind rusting scars
heaped up like silent scrap in a meadow.

## GET REAL

It will soon be time for news on TV.
Must make a cup of tea. T.S. Eliot said
*life is measured out in coffee spoons*
but let's not get sentimental. Last week,
in a lurch of worship, I began counting
the number of cups I'd drunk weekly
multiplied by months, years and decades.

I gave up when a golden chalice
asked me if I'd like to imbibe with
countless crows. Numbers are not
my thing but I do count my steps
and wrap my arms around myself
when waltzing with my own image
glaring out at me from the mirror
above the sink. Can waltzing be cured?
*Get real man,* I shout.
A buddy and I scribbled and giggled
during geometry lessons. We felt real,
half-baked primates learning to walk
in labyrinths. Today I wander among
beach towel dreams in a mirror.
Even Mouse looks puzzled as if
I was a craven relative with mileage
on the clock. I hear the beast in me
struggling with night lights and romance
knowing that whistling, saving hair
or trying to wing it in paradise is futile.
Thoughts wander – the sublime
to the high and mighty – like
laughing at nothing on a pig's back
from the top of the stairs or cheering
when a celebrant tumbles headlong
into an open grave. A bit of *craic*
you might say but the Lord's servant

might be partial to a pint or
be unfamiliar with close to the edge.

*Schadenfreude* is the word I'm after.
Imagine mawkish lads floundering
with blondes after football matches,
doing sliding tackles in takeaways
to impress lionesses out for the kill
and they dressed to the nines in
strictly out of bounds.

I like sport, watch it on telly,
go to training grounds to listen
to birds and watch feet that
never let up – chess on grass
trying to find a perfect sequence.
Daisies don't dance on digital
you might say. Well they do
but you cannot pluck them or
take them with you after dark.

I stand inside this window thinking
of an owl – like me – people dying
for rebirth – to be born into photos
of the good old days when walking
on airstreams or bathing in strings of
rain that pouted like pearls. Enough!
It will soon be time for *The News*.
That's real in a place where foreign is friend.

## WORDS COME UP SHORT

With or without the title
vibrant women can be exotic
gliding over thorn and thistle
on trusted brooms. But what
sayeth the shaman to nights
that end up in speechless confetti?
By then, it's too late for herbal tea
and only wine gets you back on
a path to harmony. Words. *Come*
*and see me on the Sabbath if you*
*want to discuss your eviction,*
sayeth the estate agent *and I'll have*
*a cynical speech prepared just for you.*
Words ignite family brawls in streets
at the expense of fondness. No need
to practise new faces. *Wipe your nose*
*you parasite. Worm. Piece of shrapnel.*

Flash Harry TV expert reports
female feet are colder than men's
and he outlines details of women
wearing the trousers over soft flesh
in a high street. Words come up short.
They come and go like promises.
Pictures are passed from head to head,
silent as space and horizons. Colours
speak in season. Scrub bushes have
more to say than words. Poems would
be up against it if it wasn't for strange talk
about mongrel hawks or witches lining up
for special offers on brooms and flying lessons.

## COVERING UP

I trawl, haul and drag up notions
to look busy, play with – to cover up.
All useless when your number's up
and you're beyond reach of
worship, flower arranging or courtship.

The world's a dark bugger of a place.
Fancy you, me, a quickstep and
a bit of jigacting on the back hills?
No. Well. Anyway, let's sing sitting
on our fat hands before coming down
with a bout of autumnal creeps.

Scattered limbs don't decompose in
hard frost and falling leaves cover
a multitude if the leaf pile's big enough.
Autumn is a time
for covering up.
Autumn is a time.
It's darker outside. Women
read crime stories. Men
look at gory stuff in film.
In epic tales, old soldiers
returned to have wounds dressed.
Odysseus rambled about
fighting one scrap after another
like a mountainy man
before returning battered and bruised
to his Penelope on Ithaca.
Closer reading suggests he was no saint.

Homer, being a busy poet,
wouldn't have had much time
for family. It is said he was
more than one person – could

have been several. Would they
or he have been buried as one?

Jesus wasn't a spark in Mary's eye
in Homer's day – before Einstein
or Hawking – before I grew up
in a confessional box where
no day went by without a sliver
of guilt to beat myself with.
At school I retreated into a void
between flagellations. I'd blast
the sky open looking to Heaven
to escape my fond body. There
was no *hey you up there* stuff.
My lips went up and down litanies
and my face freckled from gazing
upwards to worship between clouds.

Chuck me a full house of words
I'll do my best to play them up here
in the *dark*. I'm saying this as if
there was nothing out there – or is there?

## A BOAR IN BERLIN

I was almost swept off my feet
by a wild boar one morning
and me scurrying along a woodland path
in a Berlin suburb. The boar was
in a hurry – came at me from behind
like a flabbergast – swept past me
just missing my leg before disappearing
into treedom. Pork has become a four-letter word.

## My Lot

I used to believe my ancestors
were high kings. All time, hype,
courage and despair was bundled
into absorbing games – nothing
could have destroyed my dreams.
I'd pot-shot into morning mists.
My legions fought enemy tribes.
I ruled supreme until I fell asleep.
Enemies were squat, ugly and
luckless with damsels. I'd see them
running like badgers into hedges,
over distant hilltops – cowards.

Set up a monument to me, I'd cry
into my pipe dream. Battles got lost
in harsh light. I raced to manhood,
a stray wolf, blind, silent as a suite
of dislocated piano keys waiting
for a flange of fresh fingers to set
music free in an unoccupied mansion.

Before leaving, I fell to my knees
chanting softly
*there but for the grace of god go I.*

## TRANQUILITY

I unearthed a tiny segment
of quiet – once –
only to discover it was so precious
I buried it even deeper.
Awe comes and goes.
Noise is a letdown.
My greatest discovery was
getting closer to the monk in me.
I could stay put and pilgrim
to a tranquil place
where language started singing
like water serenading a balcony
in an Italian townhouse square.

Commotion seeps out of dodgy
and sacred spaces. I remember
an incident with an adventurer
in a far country where he was
conned into believing
consolation was to be had in
loud brothel music on a Sunday.
I hung about semi-hidden
in an abandoned fridge until
his tune died a natural death.
It was left to me to buy tickets
for the football. He'd seemed
set to say something but didn't.
Football is sacrament on grass.
*You daft, lazy bastard,* shouted one.
A big shout. A loud shout. How big
is a shout? How big is a daft shout?
Can it be taken apart in therapy?
Gods, bored to death on furry sofas,
don't have answers, so we might well
turn to tree limbs and garlic bread

for solace. In India they have gods
in swarms – they meditate more than most
but how do they choose a god to tune in to?

To lay his demons to rest, a loud racketeer
bawled at dinner parties: *I've weighed myself*
*and tip the scales to punch above my weight*
*and I've got evidence to prove that*
*peace and quiet is the domain of the outsider –*
*they just won't take the tablets.*

But outsiders might just be comfy people
liking an egg cosy – peaceful freaks
on magic carpets – hedonists going like
the clappers through thick and thin – might
even be crossdressers in the latest rags and Italian flair.
Walt Whitman: *we were together. I forget the rest.*

SOUP

Can a perfect sound like bubbling soup
be an image in an instant without flaw?
If I could answer such questions
I wouldn't have to pick at myself, run
fingers along railings or drum on table tops.

Perhaps a wistful Roman organist
could organise my thoughts or
a fluttering *femme fatale*
dressed up in Mata Hari flair
create lingering love lines for me.

At this moment I'm presiding over
what's left of a pot of soup I'd intended
polishing off – but that was yesterday.

*Ah, there you are, Mouse,*
*beast of the floorboards.*
*What are you grinning at?*
*Poke your fat little head back down*
*and sing for your crummy dinner.*

I sit or stand in judgement on soup.
Yesterday I was all for it. Vegetable.
Today positive broth thoughts have deserted me.

It isn't that I wouldn't eat soup, but
now I'd like something a bit chewier.
My gums are snarling, crying out
for solid stuff.

No longer in domestic mode
I head to the window to look out,
take in – absorb – smirk incognito.

I have thought of getting a black cat
but it might be into mouse flesh
and I know nothing about lifesaving.

REVERIE ON A SPREE

I'd never go to a coffee house
to discuss solid food
with a man who'd just had
teeth extracted or attempt
to elaborate on the subject
of sex change with a landlord
if I hoped to have my rent
reduced to a manageable figure.

Apropos figures. I wish you
could be at this window to see
a colourful figure serenading
a flashy peacock. The bird
seems content – must be a him.

Joking apart – fact is, city women
with classy haircuts and pets
that respond to foreign names
get all the juicy platforms. I'm
perfectly jealous – could be the
*she* in me aching for an outing but
stilettos are not the answer either,
not even in bed. Can't see myself
on a catwalk and I don't think art
does much except keep people thin.
Even clenched fists do little to
dispel the notion that thespians
hang out in secondhand clobber
and that arty friendships are
rooted in size, stature and label.

I had a literary friend who tried
to borrow a pair of my shoes for
a presentation one Sunday evening.
*Sorry. Too small.* We in-soled his

with cardboard against elements
and a master plan obliged him to
conceal his loafers under the table
during his act. I took a front seat.
The tablecloth gave cover to feet
buried and hidden as fresh coffins.

Afterwards we shambled off through
thick and thin. Thank god for dark,
said he raising a glass to the strength
of the fee to come. Ditto.

I think I'll make herbal tea.
It's time. Nettle it is.
Mug needs wash. In with teabag.
In with water. Light little flame.
Let draw. Remove teabag.
Deposit in bin. Ritual. Ritual.
Warm mug snug between hands
is good.
Have a think about the journey
of a nettle – a childhood experience
crashing face first into a colony
of stings – scorched and screaming
to mother. *You poor thing. Try these.*
Green, fat, juicy dock leaves that
didn't work but I remember the stinging.

The tea's a nice dark greenish colour,
soothing to the eye – cleans blood,
it is said. I like tea. I heard stories
of feasting on boiled nettles. Good
on them. Love boiled nettles. Grand.
Might even give me the push I need
for a walk on the wild side. I know

I'd never go to a rock concert to discuss
the effect of seawater on corns or open
a conversation with an undertaker on
shades of costume for my final outing.

Now, how did I get started on tea?
I wish I could wrap my thoughts
in a parcel of preening peacocks.

Reverie out on a spree – must be.

# HERD

The herd instinct rules the ram family.
Herd-men and herd-women,
sheep-men and sheep-women
in Botox baths,
in dark doorways to the heart of their doll's house.

A hymn to the herd.
A gaggle of pals.
A hymn to the herd.

Navy blue and grey rule in
full headlights and straight lines.

*I do girlie stuff*
*when he's not looking.*
*I do pally stuff*
*when she's not looking.*

They go to the game together
in a whirlpool of support and
do peep previews of flat stomachs
in high street shop windows.
*Hate hippy. They won't do gym*
*to insure against muscle collapse*
*and rutting breakdown* – but,
then again, my mother dressed me
in a navy suit. It suited me, she said.
I still like shades of grey in moods of blue.

## SWEATS IN AMERICA

I've heard tracksuits are called sweats
in America. Perhaps I'll head USA way
via Cuba to stock up on sensible bottoms
and there might be deals on rare bulbs
to light up my page as autumn starts
to strangle. Let's dream till our feet burn.

The auguries of longing are foolish
but cloud nine charm
lies as sweet as ever on the road ahead.

Hitching next to a funeral outfitter
on a beef burger stopover
along the Tennessee trail, I get
waylaid and horsewhipped
for dismounting in uncool sweats
and platform shoes. My nag winces
at every lash on my frail back
and jumps to my assistance with
hooves flying. It's leave in a hurry or
face a Trump-style hanging. We leave.

My mind's not right, don't you think?
Am I brainstorming a homage
to my own demise? I hope not
for I cannot disappoint my steed or
afford to dress properly for my execution.

To say clothes make the man is true
and not true. I'm bewildered
but if I am, imagine how Hamlet
must have felt about costume
when he realised it was his duty
to kill his uncle. *My prophetic soul.*

We never did get to Cuba but
I do venture out in my old bottoms
after dark
to avoid the sneer of blokes
and hissing of tomcats out of hedges.

## PROCRASTINATION

I'm back and forward to my window
watching a bean of a bloke pushing a bike
as if unsure of his next move.
A Hamlet for sure. A procrastinator.
I'd almost run down to help him if
I wasn't up here on the fourth floor.
He's probably got a puncture – leaking air.
Can't decide to cross the road or stay put.

Think things through.
Wait for the inevitable.
Think things through.

He seems to have a carpet offcut
strapped to his crossbar – readymade
for the hallway of his mother's flat.
His Ophelia would have left him.
Who'd blame her – his vehicle a bike.

He might have got a deal on the rug
but he's stranded with his bundle
and he'd be short of shillings for the bus.
Can't see him texting Mummy.

Ode to a man like all men
stuck to a spot.
Ode to a man like all men.

If that man were a well-to-do female
would I plummet down the stairs
thanking a god for dropping an opportunity
into my lap? Never look a gift horse.

The man has crossed over the street
and is standing in a shop door.

It has begun to rain. Thankfully
his life is a nightmare worth watching.

I light a candle and turn to my tea.
He's gone into my imagination.
I'll take my cup to my living room,
to the big chair. *Now there.*
The candle flickers shapes
on to the shabby wall. I wonder
if some creatures are able to tune
into voices in candle flicker.
Wallpaper looks better in this light.

Pink walls and greenish tea
and an image of a man
down there in a doorway
with a crock of a vehicle
and a lump of material
for his mother or himself.

A harmless man and
a husbandless mother
bound to each other
by a bundle. She will
turn the radio volume down
to hear the doorbell.

He's in a doorway.
How can their anxious
moments be merged
until they are reunited?
If he'd glance my way
I might weaken and share
my nettle tea.

Hamlet is duty bound to give
his mother a hiding and kill his uncle
but he bides his time – procrastinates.
*I'll put an antic disposition on,* he says.
I wonder if it would scare off money lenders.

## An Ode to Taxation

As hoarder of peeve, I often feel
like doing a modest job on the tax man.
I whistle past any hint of declaration
and don Afro hairpiece and gloves
as foil against splotch in a post box.
My sneer is loyal and recorded. Let
brown envelopes lie if lie they must.
I flaunt, toss them to flame and flush.
*Sorry candle. Sorry toilet.*
Ode to tax duties
on the tree top.
Ode to tax duties.
Tax is a case of wonder. As registered outsider
I won't declare but insiders won't either
and they rigged out in a galaxy of top gear.

Outsider: a *persona non grata*, smelly thing,
foreigner and romantic gatecrasher.
Insider: an occupant of high moral ground in
tailor-made trainers.

Both eyeball across the divide to ward off
smells or shirts stiff with starch. One group
ascribes allegiance to living artists – the other
would have them dead.
*Keep refugees out* says the insider,
*They won't pay tax.*
*Let refugees in* says the outsider,
*They won't pay tax.*

Rain throws off sparks as I sift
and sort teabags. I can't help thinking
I'm an outsider but when I trudge
and twitch with the latest version

of Homo sapiens, I seem to cross over
into regions of taking the mickey.

If all else fails, I might do a runner or
enter myself as a tax-free crowd-puller
in the Lost City of the Monkey God.

## Time Span

Time is a floating shadow
for some – for others it
means early or late when
you could be left sitting
on your tree stump
as confused as a crocodile on ice.

My friend, Mouse, is happy
with crumbs – with me
on the sports page
my fingers stroking my chin
my mind humming
the fresh air of *then,*
singing to the feel of *now.*

The buildings across this street
don't speak my language,
yet they tell me of those
who have drawn a bridge
from then till now. Past,
present, future. Family nests.

I close my eyes to see
a new generation bursting
through walls, charging
this way and that to avoid
the beaten track. The old sit
on their balconies for a
season before making way
for fresh blood hiking up
the centre of the street
in the spirit of new shops.

There's that circle again.
Children find new names

for footballers. Dads join in
for a decade and mothers
gather up tears in their stride.
Light kindling on the horizon,
bewilders for its time – then
gradually draws and burns out.
Sun peeps through rain and
smiles on cold pavements.
Trees soak up wet. Plants shed
and die. I cannot hear the voices
of the past but I know they're there
in crannies. Bedclothes drape
over balconies. Branches of families
reach out to far beyond.

An ancient warrior is a dead person.
Dead is dead as long as it's allowed
to be dead. Some, not forgotten,
have their song emblazoned in
the brick and fabric of this street.
It is my street too. I own it with
my eyes. I've got a winged horse
on my balcony and a promise of
dry land on the far horizon. My
universe embraces me where I am.
This morning an elderly couple –
two floors down –
told me they could no longer
manage the stairs.
They'd be moving to a home
in a greenbelt. *Time to go,* they said,
picking up their coats, weeping down
every last step for the last time.

Two hours later a furniture truck parked
and a young couple could be heard laughing.
It was a healthy laugh. They didn't realize
they were about to trample on a lifespan.

I see the old couple at the edge of a forest
wondering which way to turn for home.
I like the image, somehow, but it is a sad *like*.

The sun rises and sets but
it won't let us in on its secrets.

## Shall I Take Thee, Verse ...

My head's all over the place
beyond the reach of daily grind
with a bedlam brigade of
night visions and demons hot on my heels.

Fair enough, you might say but
just think of the innocent Siamese twin,
a helpless bystander
as his brother snatches
at notes in a bank.
*On my oath, Judge*
*I was on my own in Stockholm*
*at a ceremony of sorts*
*at the time of the crime.*
The judge reddens and roars.
*Which of you said that?*

If I stood on a gatepost or
beamed myself on to a chapel wall
as *Regina Coeli*
would I sell enough raffle tickets
to buy a hotel with Cana flair for
the best of wedding feasts yet to come?

To get off the ground and keep afloat,
I could offer levitation lessons
for beginners – be an outlet for grails
and tours on versions of sainthood
and nothing but sainthood. Amen.
No, that would never work.
I'd end up wriggling, scratching,
and denied my rights in taverns.

Verse is reasonably constant.
Shall I take thee, verse, as my
lawful companion? Say yes, please.

Verse is rhythm, isn't it?
Verse is song, isn't it?
Verse is rhythm, isn't it?

I hope to sing the length
of my borrowed life. I could
opt to eat less, measure
results in my waistline
but the distance my song
takes me doesn't depend
on my choice of nutrition
only – for when all is said
and done, I'll be placed in
a cold crypt out of season.

I could suggest a cosy nest
but when my struggle stops,
shouting is futile. Now,
I don't wish to create unrest
but my last request would be
to be planted very low under
all others – very low where
rival spirits and demons
could interview me without
fear of last rites spoiling the fun.

I'm a drumbeat in abandoned streets
and forlorn meadows
who'll have to face the music
when that hermit heart beckons.

For now, I am up here
on my fourth floor island.
The woman next door
has just closed her door
gently. I don't know her
but when she sings
she's got a soothing voice.
Shall I take thee, verse …

## MOONSOME

It's still evening in a hint of night.
I recall a wise person telling tales
of the man in the moon
and a little boy crying out
*there really has been a man
on the moon.* The boy was right.
His time is ahead and with it
imaginings are disappearing
into digital rage. Hard drives
whisper to hard drives.
Hard drives drive hard bargains.
Moonbeams pour streams of light
on shut-down towns – on brambles
that creak and whisper. A black cloud
surprised one of my moons,
gobbled it up and took it from me.
I knew it was still up there
but neither pleading nor nightmare
let me back into its aura. I recall
a perfect moment in a spring field.
I'm in that field again – in a fairy *rath*
among beech arms straining upwards.

I've still got my mug of tea,
my Aladdin lamp in a cave.
I have avoided the sorcerer
so far. Moments of magic
don't try to escape – hilltops
jut up through fog in moonlight
and my tea makes me lively and rich.

Imagine the following
in fast forward: a head
that can't stop thoughts
is perched at the window

of a fourth floor flat.
Its keeper looks out to
the city, slithering about
hoping for a storyline.

In an Aesop fable, a burglar fox
was rummaging among possessions
in a performer's room when
it came upon a mask – a replica
of a human head – *a fine head*
it said – *pity it doesn't have a brain.*
The performer had left without his head.

Do I exist in my dream?
If I stroke my head
with a wand of moon dreams,
will I find myself in a cave
with a magic lamp
cupped in my two hands?
It's a deep cup,
a sacred goblet containing
all the ghosts I believe in.

It draws a dark curtain
across men in uniform,
women in servitude,
fear etched into frowns
of children as far from
magic caves
as our self-made gods
are from our galaxies.

## CHILDREN ARE WISE

High priests and politicians
are out of place
in fields where songbird chimes.
And, besides, big bishops
look bizarre in bars and open air
after a life of walking from
one mansion to another
oiling their fat hands *ad infinitum.*
*Suffer little children to come unto me.*
Oh, oh, here we go again!
*And we'll starve you if we have to.*
*Amen.*
*I know you are hungry, child*
*so let us break sacred bread and*
*offer it up. I know you are hungry, child.*

I haven't checked post today
so I'll amble down
the seventy-four steps
fully clothed incognito.
Perhaps there's an offer
on a sprig of sprays
in my mailbox to keep me
tuned to the latest smells.

You can never be sure
of the human-in-people
when it comes out to play.
Political figures are in thrall
to spray sounds, purring motors
and dumbing down.
*Why all the straight lines, sir,*
the child asks?
Powers-that-be retort: *hack*
*nature down to the wishbone,*

*give it war talk. Laboratories*
*do your job, find solution to*
*the misery of seasonal growth.*
*There must be a poison to keep*
*hedges brown all year round.*
*How else can we expect*
*to stay in power? Rise up men,*
*take control of upbringing.*
*Wildlife must be tamed or eradicated.*

Innocent scrub and hedgerows
turn away embarrassed by
trims and cuts imposed on them.
*We're all in a straight line now, Sir.*

Ghandi was a politician.
He was a wise man – a child.
He did good in his time.
When Martin Luther King
was murdered,
the world stared at barricades.
Nelson Mandela lit a fire
and taught people to dance.

I'm not a philosopher, but know
that a new set of racing tyres
or the shape of a hairdo
have less to do with wisdom
than we are led to believe.

I watched three school children
stroll along in deep discussion.
They seemed engrossed and cosy
in their winter gear – like snails
with an onus of adult dread

pegged to their backs – dread
to be shed in a lifetime – hopefully.

Let's not teach anymore. Let's listen.
Gather up the bliss and thrills of youth,
go to the fields to be young again. Look
for legends in pools of light under rocks.

Let children enjoy dancing as long
as grass is grass. Shut down facts.
Waken to wild displays along slopes.
Leave systems to the pale faces of those
who can't live without.

## A Two Woman Giggle

Two women planted themselves
deep in bulging crops.
*There's a grand bite to that beetroot*
said one
*but look at that bugger of a bird*
*winking down at us,* said the other.
*That's life,* said the first, seeing red.
One had an auntie who
didn't leave her hillside cot
for twenty years, and when she did
she rode about on a beast
wearing nothing but a cheeky smile.
She loved gypsy music.
One October she returned to her bed
for good.
The other claimed to have noble forefathers
who disliked creatures that wouldn't wag a tail
when they stepped down from their high horses.

The two women giggled going
round the corner to their snug.
At the door, one sniggered,
*but beetroot is red.*
*Indeed, and mushrooms are magic*
giggled the other
and in they went twittering
like a pair of truants on the make.

## PROPER JOB

There's nothing outside my window
but a street of houses – lines old
and new – lines beaming on a page.
If I stood at this window for
twenty years, would work stand still?
Do holy men and women work?
Could a druid be a good goalkeeper?
*There are more things in*
*heaven and earth, Horatio ...*
Sitting in a train, a loud man
roared, *my son must work hard*
*to get a top job, to keep him right,*
*straight and narrow.* His wife,
unsure of straight and narrow,
chanted she'd consult her shaman
at eventide. He bellowed,
*there are so many proper jobs*
*and our son's only wish is to*
*study that waster, Plato. Get him*
*into Revenue and he'll be right for life.*

Crowds gathered behind a favourite.
His gang was huge and rough.
Her few gentle souls gave way
and stepped down at the next stop.

His followers shouted, *up work,*
*long live muck spreaders and*
*weed killer.* He ordered a round
of Schnapps with pork chunks
proclaiming that life without
a proper job was an existence
for shirkers and dossers.

*Feck reading,* a small fat man hissed.
*Bet you snore,* a corpulent woman shrieked.
*Middle finger to fiction,* a baldy one bawled.
*Let god take care of climate,* caterwauled another.
*Hear, hear* rattled along the carriage.

The train accelerated in waves of excitement.
Word got about and swallows shared opinion
on the train top. The wife of the man who
believed in work booked her fragile followers
into a refresher course she'd be facilitating
on the influence of Oriental meditation
on popular culture. She adored bank notes
but kept it to herself. She had principles,
never spoke about cash and dressed accordingly.

Cows in fields got wind of something,
looked up bovinely, but didn't stop eating.

## No Escape

I try to keep the prattle of death
at arm's length – it rattles and rots,
seasonal as seeds – no escape.

From this perfect perch I see
holiday gravestones floating
on a landscape like draughts in
a dead ancestor's drawing room.

Here I am, a subdivision of
Homo erectus – a chunk of
wrack and ruin, afraid to take
a dip or head off at the clifftop
before the push and even if
I could swim I'd be lost and
if I had a car it would hum,
spit out poison and take up space.
The hummingbird hums and glides,
frogs croak their needs and
all of nature lays out its carpet.
Landscapes, hillsides and valleys
won't obey and be still – while
the economic agenda rumbles on
with perfect bullets and landmines.

Mountain, let the moon drop light
on you. Don't smother your heart
in grief. Let rainwater heal life
into your soft seams and
winds airbrush wounds we inflict.
On clear nights stars huddle
to decry the mess we strew
or they smoulder in anger as
untidy clouds drape in slurps.

## In Vino Veritas

I haven't moved much in the past few hours:
kitchen to living room to window
to armchair – to out of touch – to enough,
so let's wander from horizon to horizon.

I have a nice bottle of Merlot to help
travel beyond pesky inhibitions.
A glass or two should level my hills.
I can visit clay sculptures on cloud nine,
or listen to a nightingale
serenade a dew-coated sunflower
and I can do it from my perch out of harm's way.

Outside is a void – not a centre of lavish.
I have my sweet bottle in my hand
and an eager glass. *Ah, yes, the opener.*
Now my bloodstream's awake.
My heart's on fire. *In Vino Veritas.*
Well here I am, back in my armchair
about to open a bottle. That done
I'll tackle pouring. Executed.
Cheers Mouse. My glass half empty.
A little sip. Half full. Delight,
Half empty. I am the product of
elements – mostly water – and
with water of life on my palate,
I'm as content as a stray donkey
among thistles. What's the sense
of coming and going when you can
travel on wine. Vines turn grapes
into a jamboree of tint and binge.
If I can't find pleasure, I hope it finds me.
This vintage is wholesome. I'll have another.
In for a penny, in for a pound. Right.

I'm as cosy and free as a wisp.
I sit by a riverbank with
an ornament of a creature
promising pleasure. I pluck
a flower, imbibe and immerse
in the moment. Dusk falls
into the empty air. Dogs
bark out of sight and heaven
means nothing to a tipsy man
in an armchair. I pray for a mirage,
loiter by my riverbank rose
and if a kind of paradise is
tacked on at the end, well and good.

Shadows in wine and twilight
swallow up tears.
Shadows in wine and twilight.

*Tell me a story, tell me a story,*
*tell me a story and then I'll go to bed.*
It seems so long ago. *You promised me*
*you said you would – tell me a story and*
*then I'll go to bed.* I remember
the river seemed pleased – it
had rained in rainlets. I cast
into the lazy water and had
a perch in an instant. The water
winked. We were easy together.
My fish struck out aimlessly
with its little glistening fins.
In vain. One blunt thwack and
it was done. Bagged. The hook
was rescued like a drowning parable.
I had just the one hook and line
attached to my lean hazel rod.

The search for slender worms
was a litany housed in a jam jar
and nurtured like a rich relative.

My great fear was eel. It swallowed
hook, line and sinker and wriggled
like a schoolboy hiding from the truth.
I'd peep at my catch
thinking of a fish family torn apart,
a mother ripped asunder at feeding time.

Fish are silent. Don't feel pain,
says the angler. They fidget a bit
and are still. *Eat up your fish …*
*tell me a story and then*
*I'll go to bed.* It's into autumn.
Trees are haggard showing age
like ones that have had enough.
The breeze is soft. A fisherman
with rod, baits, flies and waders
nods and ambles past
in that fisherman way. I look down
at my makeshift tackle and weep.
Tears need to free themselves.

I select a worm sleek as seal,
cast and snatch a sparkling pike
drowning in the limp evening air.
Even glum grass is in despair as
I pack up under a canopy of thorn
and briar. The pike stretches out wings
inviting me to hop on to its back. I do,
euphoric, fearless flying higher
and higher above shrouds of houses.

What's this? I must have nodded.
Dozed. A noddy, noddy forty winks.
My glass half empty. Ah well.
I've been as triumphant as
any fisher boy bearing gifts
of sweet fish but there's no
trace of me on the dark skyline.
I must have overshot our house
and disappeared. To where?
Here? And in between?

## SPRING

But spring will come again.
Grass will be greener
and pleased.
Hills will arch, stretch
and spread blankets
of colour.
Trees will stop mourning.
They'll lilt.
Humans will feel warmer,
doff, peel, shed and season.
Doors close. Doors open.

I'll breathe plumes into twilight
and be easy. Robins and wrens
will come again to garnish branches.
They'll chorus and sing to high fields,
low lands, dykes and pastures as
fox cubs and kittens tackle first frolics.

I've had my fill of drear,
I think – as my kettle screams
like a lone voice on a fresh planet.

## BLISSFUL ROAD

It's time on the road that counts
before that final crossing
to where a grim gentleman waits.
I'll face him on proud horseback
and hope he's not another illusion
designed to shatter innocent hope.

In the meantime, I've got junk mail
in my phone, storerooms of notions
and only myself to fight with.
What I'm trying to say is that
if I can't negotiate the fog, I want
to leave this life without reckless hope
of a sloppy space in Paradise Cloud.

Grasses are silent. Water is sombre
and still. The kettle has boiled.
I'm dressed simply in pyjamas.

Man is journeyman, part domestic,
part alien, part flower in season
and part furious corncrake
losing its voice to selfish gratification,
robbing us of nature's warm embrace.

A good friend gave up teaching.
He was no longer allowed
to take his pupils to search
for unsorted life under stones.
The message was simple:
trust steam, trust cloud,
stay indoors, avoid rash
and count your lucky gold bars.

Stay indoors – trust steam.
Hillside haze is outdated.
Stay indoors – trust steam.

I recall seeing and hearing
a blissful woman driving her cow
in the summer air on a river road.

Old pictures in green patchwork
taunt me. These pictures shaped me.

## Auntie's Car

One day, before the global scavenger
began to rummage and scan, my auntie
asked me to take her Fiat-something
to the garage. Hardly started without
prayer on Monday. I got to the garage
with a semi-flat to boot. Not rimmed.
Relief. *Come back at four.* I did. Had
to hang about for an hour – saw that
plugs were new – *the old ones?* I
posing with one elbow on the roof
like the swanky fella in the showroom.
No man admits to pain in a garage.
*Start her up.* I did.
*Sounds fine,* as if I knew what to listen for.
*You're a bit dear,* parting with auntie's cash.
Proper talk. I was all bloke making my way.
*I'll dip her while I'm at it.*
*Wouldn't do any harm, I suppose.* He did.
*She's grand – gave the wheels a few shots,*
*a leaking valve was all you had.*
A leaking valve
was all I had!
*Jesus Maria.*
I steamed out of the *cul-de-sac*
with the man looking at me piloting
an ageing Fiat – could be my topcoat
he was eyeing up. I was proud of
that garment. Safely parked, I was met
with a smile and a tea from the top shelf.
Even back then I didn't add sugar.

## FROM MY PLINTH

Sometimes I imagine
I can hear my ancestors
trying to see each other
in a fresh light – repairing
old discord beyond reach
of silly politics and high
moral ground.
Past, present and future
seem spliced into images
of generations gliding
from day to day as if
all that was needed was
a quiet corner
to pull the pieces together.

It's almost dark. I hear gulls
and agitated voices in the street
below.
My ancestors sleep in my head.
If I woke them one by one,
they might tell of bare feet
on pebbles after school.
I can see one relative smile
at central heating and a fat one
that liked food but didn't let on.

Fibs and fabrications filter down to us
in clickedy clackedy time
chirping in flashes like cricket song.

I walked stone paths, muddy fields,
fairy trails shrouded in crab apples
and hawthorn berries – my tender feet
coating in the hard skin of journeying.

A palate of birds, hares, badgers
and questions we didn't ask
added to my watery landscape
when swinging on an iron gate.

The dream, visible between trees,
was skimpy and far away. I'd
have to go there one day. I did.

I'm here, far from that unkempt,
briary patch, bandaged horizons
and stars that fell one by one.

Some stars are melodies. Others
threaten to carry me off.
As evening fades, I turn inwards.

## RAVENS ARE DARK

I'm creating my world bit by bit.
It's an enormous balloon falling
upwards on its way down to earth.
I puff and puff till I blush, crimson
as a teenager caught in the act – afraid
to stop in case my dream collapses
into the comings and goings of fate.

I try to imagine the plight of a groom
washed up on a remote island on
his wedding day. The ferryman leaves.
The tide is rising. The bride
gets fed up waiting and flits off.
A scavenger cracks up laughing,
knowing there'll be a feast if
it hangs about. The tabloids are
overjoyed when the bride promises
to sleep by the seashore and sing
a love song she'd write that very night.
The dark eyes of ravens are smirking.

## AT ONE

I take a chair to my kitchen window
to watch the game of light
refracting on twilight zones
and beaming into openings
to the natural world. Outside
there are city versions of
wildlife at large but way beyond
a boy floats in a cradle of stillness.
He is singing of faraway places
from his remote hilltop
while rabbits, lambs and foxes
skit in the breeze.
The moon singles itself out.
The city stares up in awe.
Quiet falls like snoozing frost.
A taxi hums. It's all singing
and parrot-like dancing. Beams
arrange themselves on children
twisting, turning, dropping their
sunflower eyelids. I am not here
to unravel, solve or give answers.
I am here, a slumberer wondering
if one can remain in thrall to sound
as a beam wraps up for the night.

There were times when I considered
a pact with Mephisto
but no one has seen hell and
I have no faith in the Garden of Eden
where a woman up a ladder plucks apples
and a man in shrubbery peeps up.
Some say she was a right one, but this
was before agony columns or cars.

Much later a carpenter, his wife, their baby,
wise men and a donkey added romance.
We had a new god and a gutful of guilt
to help keep our actions in check.

I could drink the nectar of the unbeliever
and kneel before stuffed craven crows,
pots of tea and fairytales – even be
a player in a flat with a mouse
to protect me from wily gods
that shape life and seem to botch it.
Tabernacles to the unknown test my resolve.

I trust in windows and beyond. Let's share
this cauldron of moonbeams and ashes.
Thoughts, thinking.
I am you and you are me.
We waltz on horseback
like circus folk
like a brown leaf in autumn
like an real estate flier
as if we were at one.

BLUE

Life is a hard won beauty and
even if we share common ground
it keeps shifting.
I feel blue.
You feel blue.
Do we feel the same blue?
I like blue because I can wallow
and sink into blue marrow
be part of an empire of stone.
I could be a blue-blood type
wearing a homemade crown
lording over lunacy
rummaging for horns
to confirm my supremacy in rutting season.
Colour is a far country
in the tight grip of moonbeams.
I wonder if dogs see blue or
if they pray. They have memory
when they look at us
in that doggy way but
do they kneel to a canine goddess
before dog-parading contests?

Starlings couldn't possibly think
and fly at the same time – or
perhaps they can as they
sculpt their colours in a blue sky.
Only the heart can respond.

## THE CARDINAL AND THE SHOVEL

Fantasy is all mine. Time is all mine.
Come late wind. Come early wind.

Ministering angels deserve a smile
but when a shovel-bearing cardinal
takes a seat in my favourite café
all senses are tested for self deception.

The anointed one whispers
to his companion
suggesting maverick or bonkers.

His shovel's label is intact
and its head is free of mud.
There might be a plan
to put it to work: get
into grave digging,
drumming up business
among pensioners?
Snigger. Torrents outside.
No day for digging.

*Two coffees and two cakes please*
in a hollow cathedral voice.
Is he expecting a second coming?
God not dead after all!

A resurrection, hallucination or mirage
is out of the question in this weather.
Promoters need a semblance of sun and
sand to sell the pilgrim path to Mount Shangri-La.
All certainties are questioned as the
cardinal gathers his secret illusions
and faces into a hell of a downpour
with one coffee and one cake untouched.

# CONVERSATIONS WITH SELF

I'm up here. Mouse is not in on this.
Dusk is coming down in strobes
with hints of light circling and
refracting on bins, buckets and bikes.

I'll go for a walk a little later
when evening has settled.
I'd love to see the streets
through the eyes of another.
There might be mysteries in
their vision – more goblins at large.

The nag in me is a stray.
I want to nibble and ramble
into circles with self.
I say it again – into circles
with self.
I languish in my bloodstream
and rub my eyes raw to see
if I can sense the childhood
I left before it left me.
I hedge by it, reach out my hand
but we no longer connect.
I write but I was a better poet
in days when I'd look into
pools to see dark portends
bubbling up. Wistful yearning
in a fourth floor flat – if nothing else.

Thanks are due to all who have supported me through my years of writing: publishers Alan Hayes of Arlen House. Olaf Hille of Blaupause Books, Ernst Klett Verlag, I am indebted to Live Encounters where some of these poems have been published.

I'd like to express my sincere thanks to those who have read and advised me on this collection: Ian Watson, Ger Reidy, Sean Walsh, John Corless, Sally McKenna and, especially, to Joanna who trusts my instinct as I do her unerring judgement. My brothers and sisters attend my readings when they have more pressing business to occupy their time. Thanks to national and international schools, universities and colleges, Eily Vaughan, Brendan Flynn at Clifden Arts Festival, Poetry Ireland, Hamburger Autorenvereinigung, Kennys Galway, Castle Bookshop Castlebar, NDR Hamburg, Mayo Arts Office, Dagmar Wennmacher and Johanna Blum in Germany, Claremorris Townhall Theatre, Over the Edge, Libraries, especially Mayo and Galway, Joe Byrne and Midwest Radio, Jho and Sinead at All Points West, Joachim Matschoss and friends in Melbourne, John Duffy in Bonn, Geoff Gates in Sydney, Ballina Arts Centre, All Points West Media Services, The Irish Embassy in Berlin, friends and acquaintances in Hamburg, Ireland and other corners of the world.

# ABOUT THE AUTHOR

Terry McDonagh, from Cill Aodáin, Kiltimagh, lives in Mayo and in Germany. His poetry collections include: *The Road Out, A World Without Stone; Boxes; A Song for Joanna; Cill Aodáin and Nowhere Else; In the Light of Bridges – Hamburg Fragments; The Truth in Mustard; Ripple Effect; Echolocation; Lady Cassie Peregrina.*

Terry taught English at the University of Hamburg, was Drama Director at the International School Hamburg for 15 years and has facilitated residencies in Europe, Asia and Australia. His poem, 'Out of the Dying Pan into the Pyre', was longlisted for The Poetry Society poetry prize 2015 and 'From a Hauptbahnhof Café in Berlin' was highly commended in the Gregory O'Donoghue prize 2016.

In 2017 he was Artistic Director of WestWords, Germany's first Irish literature festival in Hamburg. He's been narrator and acting voice in several RTÉ Junior dramas. Twelve of his poems have been put to music for voice and string quartet by the late composer Eberhard Reichel in Hamburg. He has been featured in the newspaper, *Hamburger Abendblatt* and on German radio and TV on many occasions.

Other books include: *I wanted to bring you Flowers/ich kann das alles Erklaeren* (drama) – Fischer Aachen; *One Summer in Ireland* (fiction) – Klett Stuttgart; *Elbe Letters go West/Briefe von der Elbe* – Blaupause; *Michel the Merman*, a story for young people based on Hamburg legends (illustrated by Mark Barnes NZ) – BOD Hamburg; *Tiada Tempat di Rawa* (translation into Indonesian); *Kiltimagh* – Blaupause (translation into German by poet Mirko Bonné).

www.terry-mcdonagh.com